DATE DUE

Electricians

by Mary Firestone

Consultant:
Robert W. Baird
Vice President
Apprenticeship and Training, Standards and Safety
Independent Electrical Contractors, Inc.

Bridgestone Books
an imprint of Capstone Press
Mankato, Minnesota

Bridgestone Books are published by Capstone Press
151 Good Counsel Drive, P.O. Box 669, Mankato, Minnesota 56002
http://www.capstone-press.com

Library of Congress Cataloging-in-Publication Data
Firestone, Mary.
    Electricians/by Mary Firestone.
    p. cm.—(Community helpers)
    Includes bibliographical references and index.
    ISBN 0-7368-0956-2
    1. Electricians—Juvenile literature. 2. Electric engineering—Juvenile literature. [1.
    Electricians. 2. Occupations.] I. Title. II. Community helpers (Mankato, Minn.)
TK148 .F52 2002
621.319'24'023—dc21   00-012542

Summary: A simple introduction to the work electricians do, the tools they use, the people who
    help them, and their importance to the communities they serve.

Editorial Credits
Sarah Lynn Schuette, editor; Karen Risch, product planning editor; Linda Clavel, designer;
    Heidi Schoof, photo researcher

Photo Credits
Arthur Tilley/FPG International LLC, 8
Capstone Press/Gary Sundermeyer, 14, 16
David F. Clobes, Stock Photography, cover, 10, 12, 20
Rubberball Productions, 6
Shaffer Photography/James L. Shaffer, 4
Visuals Unlimited/Jeff Greenberg, 18

**Bridgestone Books thanks Shawn Hilgers, Frank Hilgers, Ted Clavel, and Brian Dols for
    providing props for photographs in this book.**

1 2 3 4 5 6 07 06 05 04 03 02

Table of Contents

Electricians

Electricians help make electricity safe to use. Lights, computers, and other machines need electricity to work. Electricity moves through wires. Electricians put wires together. They install wires in places that need electricity.

install
to put something in place

What Electricians Do

Electricians read blueprints. Blueprints show where wires go in a building. Electricians then install wires, outlets, and light switches. They also test, fix, and replace wires that have worn out.

outlet
a place where items are plugged in and connected to electricity

Where Electricians Work

Electricians work in many places. They work indoors in homes and buildings. They work outdoors on streetlights and stoplights. Electricians also work at construction sites and factories. Some electricians work for power companies.

Types of Electricians

Construction electricians put wiring into new buildings. Maintenance electricians check wires to make sure they are working correctly. Some electricians work outdoors on power lines.

Tools Electricians Use

Electricians use pliers to twist the ends of wires together. They also use wire cutters. Electricians use meters to check wires. They use ladders and cranes to reach high places.

meter
a machine used to test the amount of electricity moving through wires

What Electricians Wear

Electricity is dangerous. Electricians often wear long-sleeved shirts and pants to protect themselves from shocks and burns. They also wear safety gloves, boots, safety glasses, and hard hats.

shock
the sudden effect of an electrical current going through someone's body

15

How Electricians Learn

Electricians learn their job by going to school and by working as an apprentice. Apprentices take classes to learn how electricity works. They also work with a master electrician to learn to do the job correctly.

master electrician
an electrician with many years of experience

People Who Help Electricians

Architects design buildings and draw blueprints for electricians to follow. Inspectors make sure electricians install wires correctly. Electricians help each other by working together on projects.

How Electricians Help Others

Electricians help people use electricity safely. They work to make sure people have power during and after storms. They install wires for fire alarms and medical equipment. Electricians also fix broken wires.

Hands On: Make Static Electricity

Static electricity is one form of electricity that you can make by rubbing things together.

What You Need

Small fluorescent light bulb
Sock

What You Do

1. Turn the lights off.
2. Rub the sock against your hair very quickly.
3. Put the sock on one end of the fluorescent bulb.

Tiny bits of light should appear in the bulb. Try rubbing the sock faster and longer. Put the sock on the bulb again. What happens?

Words to Know

apprentice (uh-PREN-tiss)—a person who learns a skill by going to school and by working with a skilled person

architect (AR-ki-tekt)—a person who designs buildings and draws blueprints

blueprint (BLOO-print)—a detailed plan for a project or an idea; blueprints show electricians where to install wires, switches, and outlets.

electricity (e-lek-TRISS-uh-tee)—a form of energy used to power lights and other machines

wire (WIRE)—a long, thin piece of metal; electricity moves through wires.

Read More

Dann, Sarah. *The Science of Energy.* Living Science. Milwaukee: Gareth Stevens, 2000.

Stille, Darlene R. *Electricity.* Simply Science. Minneapolis: Compass Point Books, 2001.

Thomas, Mark. *A Day with an Electrician.* Hard Work. New York: Children's Press, 2000.

Internet Sites

Atoms Family–Electrical Safety
http://www.miamisci.org/af/sln/frankenstein/safety.html
EIA Kid's Site
http://eia.doe.gov/kids/
What Does An Electrician Do?
http://www.whatdotheydo.com/electric.htm

Index